AMONG 2700 ACRES

ONLY 640 ACRES

ARE FILLED WITH

MICROENCAPSULATION,

MACROENCAPSULATION,

AND DIRECT LANDFILL

AHSAHTA PRESS

BOISE, IDAHO
2018

THE NEW SERIES #85

A**A*A*A

HEIDI LYNN STAPLES

Ahsahta Press, Boise State University, Boise, Idaho 83725-1580
Cover design by Quemadura
Book design by Janet Holmes
ahsahtapress.org

LIBRARY OF CONGRESS CATALOGING-IN-PUBLICATION DATA

Names: Staples, Heidi Lynn, 1971- author.
Title: A**A*A*A / Heidi Lynn Staples.
Description: Boise, Idaho : Ahsahta Press, Boise State University, [2018] |
    Series: The new series ; #85
Identifiers: LCCN 2018001118| ISBN 9781934103814 (paperback : alk. paper) |
    ISBN 1934103810 (paperback : alk. paper)
Classification: LCC PS3619.T368 A6 2018 | DDC 811/.6—DC23
LC record available at https://lccn.loc.gov/2018001118

ACKNOWLEDGMENTS

Thank you to the University of Alabama for supporting the travel necessary to this
manuscript through CARSCA and RGC research grants;

thank you to the editors of *Denver Quarterly, Duniyaadaari, Open Letters,* and *Verdad*
for publishing poems from the manuscript;

thank you to Janet Holmes, for her vision, her example, her fierce generosity;

thank you to my daughter, Sophie, whose sense of adventure and love for all creatures
helped inspire this book; and thanks to her dad, who tended the homefires while we
were away with the faeries . . .

CONTENTS

IV.   FRUITY DEPARTURES

FOR JOHN AND SOPHIE

"Where Thou art—that—is Home—"

I. ALL WEEDS HAVE IN COMMON

Walking the path, I stop to pick up
bleached bark from a tree, curled into
a scroll of ancient wisdom I am unable to read.

A**A*A*A OF THE INDIGO SNAKE

Audubon Birmingham Mountain Workshop

≈

U ancient mouth ≈ black & blue ≈ old blood-lidded motherer

Drymarchon ≈ lore of the forest floor ≈ longing's figure
from whose back have you leapt cord striking a chord, along my
neck of the woods is ripples ≈ Wet fore ≈ living shiver?

We R place≈to≈place when supple lifted up out of
the plastic ark nest ≈ draped a ground my small daughter

Let me touch ≈ let me hold ≈ give me give me it it it

≈

≈

≈

≈

night this a longleaf pine echo cistern   ≈ slit frm fire
ground grackle coal rivulets streams dreams-n-glades seams
trees forest gives rush ≈ we have taken yr vein in name

Wet's knot rephrased from R casual racer erasure
Let me touch ≈ let me hold ≈ get meat get means it it it
in R wake ≈ wake ⬆ to what's ⬇ ≈ who's the snake in the grass?

≈

≈

≈

≈

≈

≈

DUST

Dust is the only secret from the grate's breath. Dust an unseamed presence the
   lights at night flare in the house, house whose windows are eyes to the sole
   body, mine, whispers of dust spilled everywhere throughout.

The cabinets and dresses shushed and vieled by dust, these bodies unbecoming
   wide-spread public unrecorded, can you see their eyes?

In the morning, when I dust off the piano, I see a park of single-wides
   shipwrecked on bricks porches empty blinds drawn everyone inside. They
   begin to sing, first softly then loudly a unison wafts out of the keyholes
   rising song of dust, dust from the ground and breathed what an orchestra
   dust and odors from the landfill

dust, clouds of
toxic dust singing
from its half-dozen
coal ash ponds

The song is in parts
soft like a dump
uncovered then loud
in mounds stacked six
stories high, trembling
trouble notes a mere
100 feet from

On my piano, dust and dust odors. I tap my feet to the tune while I dust
   stirring up dust health problems, dust respiratory illness dust headaches
   dust dizziness dust nausea dust vomiting.

The children come in from the street. Their voices burn the morning is too
   joy, mix with the dust lakes of particulate makes sky a pyre, even as the
   landfill is song. Please let me dust in peace, I say. They go to pieces, the
   children, giggled with gladness, devoted to all things lively and dancing.
   Children come to us nude from the whirl to the world, every cell a swell
   unstill always a time for dancing. They cannot help themselves.

dust lust lustrous dust rust rest test testicular vehicular homicidal dust the dust
   sings its voice carries everywhere err on the air

dusts are inhaled, they transport us

I see the children bright-winged anemics in all their vast array, holding hands
   in my living room, they cannot help themselves, their bodies sing-a-long
   instruments and organs as their brains swell, light on their feet as dust
   clouds and odors

When I open the front door, they go dancing down the lane, enchanted
   humming dust's tune as full of mischief as fugitive ash.

Here, O here

cashes to cashes
lust to dust
in trust we dust

I call out to them to stop watch for clouds of toxic dust, remember the landfill
   that rises 110 feet above the floor of the high desert

Yet the song fills every crevice and steals blown open the children's mouths, the
   street like a god's intestinal track pocked with ulcers, their bodies dance
   and sing dust they cannot help themselves every hole the song is pores
   into the lane dancing through the neighborhood's homes, cars and gardens,
   waifs wafting asthmatic breathing polyrhythmically percussive rising as
   the rotten egg stench of hydrogen sulfide dust permeated dust houses dust
   life dust dusting dust

See how the children dance into the side of the mountain.
Coal dust, the future is theirs, dust is the only secret?

BLACKBIRD FIGURES IN A LAKE GETAWAY

Prewitt Hill Slave Cemetery, Northport, Alabama

I

Among 300-500 buried slaves,
The hand over the mouth of the thing
Was the lake getaway.

II

We were reminded of the back of our minds,
Like a slave graveyard
Beside a lake getaway

III

The getaway had to have everything, the wife wanted laundry, a dishwasher…
It had [been] gotten out of hand[s].

IV

A man and a wife
Are a plantation.
A man and a wife and a lake getaway
Are a plantation.

V

I do not know what I hear,
The crush of leaves under our feet,
Or the ghost of Miss Betsy in her white dress helping
Them. The sound of the lake getaway good to the slaves
Or *coo who coo who coo who.*

VI

Marked graves fill the earth
With the Prewitt family.
Not all slaves in the lake getaway:
Father Wilson Prewitt
April 13, 1864–October 22, 1936
The letters
Etched in the stone
A law of dominion.

VII

What happened to John Prewitt after the Civil War?
Well, I don't know.
What happened to the slaves after the Civil War? Were they allowed to stay on
    here?
Well, I don't know.

VIII

I like to believe in a blank slate
And it's dear the elderly white man who built a lake getaway with his wife
    Margie out here, his straw hat, his kayak, his neighbor's dog Charlie thinks
    he owns this place
But I believe, too,
That the lake getaway lies
In what I like to believe

IX

He give them this land to bury their . . .
You couldn't walk out here a year ago,
A Boy Scout come out,
The whole history of it in Miss Eloise's scrapbook,
There on the back of that red car

X

At the site of the lake getaway
Spectacular in the sunset
This one's pretty interesting, it's got a heart carved on it
Blessed are the pure at heart
Gone to rest
In Memory of
A blank slate
A blank slate
A blank slate
A blank slate
Born a blank slate
Died a blank slate
Banked, lived in the blank, slated to slave

A blank slate
A blank slate
The blank slates reveal
A field with lungs
Are they holding their breath?
Can they breathe?
Are they sails filled with ire
On a slow boat to justice
Or is this a wreck run aground?
A blank slate a fist shaken still
A blank slate a blank face
A blank face a black face
A back turned a block burned
A blank, a black, a block
Blocked, blocked, blocked
On the block
On the block
On your back
Hands over your head
Hounds, hounds, hounds,
By the body and the blood,
Whose blank slate?

XI

We've come here to figure,
Solving nothing,
Dissolving for x.
Daniel trips in a hole
Katy sits on the lake's edge
Meredith sits on the lake's edge
Spencer stands on the periphery
Brett paces the periphery
Carter bends down
Jordan steps over and Jordan steps
It was seven white graduate students with their white professor driving into
this neck of the woods like when they came in here with sonar equipment to
see what's down there
past the blank slates.

8

XII

The waters have been rising.

The lake getaway may be eroding.

XIII

It was yesterday enslaved dressed in all white driven down the middle of
Tuscaloosa to work in Mobile today.

It was a gate and a welcome.

The lake getaway lies at the end of Old Byler Road, oldest public road in
Alabama.

A**A*A*A OF THE YELLOWHAMMER

√

like some festoon from the American Civil War
how yo√ carry on & on atop a pole, *#yarr√p*
#wake-√p walk-√p wick-√p as in yo√'re s√ch a pecker

√

√   √□

#harry-wicket heigh-ho ≈ not m√ch depends on a willf√l
sparrow ≈ known as a devil bird scribble lark ≈ low form
w/ a pl√me & the √mbrage to cop√late on a

√√
$\overline{}$
√

high wire ≈ yo√'re √nbalanced and in a delicate state
yo√'re biodiverse is america's amazon
yo√'re bloody national conflict & its aftermath

√

how to find a hope's simple in your fecal sack,
to la√d yo√r mother how she pl√cks clean the heir's an√s
that's as gross as the asphalt factory with toxic d√mp
rhyming with the train ha√ling nat√ral gas #th√mp th√mp th√mp?

√ √ √□

THE MANAGER

Chem Waste; Emelle, Alabama--largest hazardous waste site in the U.S.

What you have heard is not quite true. We were welcomed at the site. The
PR person greeted us with a handshake, the guard waved us in. There were
notebooks, posters about hierarchies of waste management, a conference table.
He offered us water, soda, an analogy. It was everything you have on your
kitchen sink, we have here. It was all the products we all enjoy. It was all you
girls paint your nails, acetone. You all use Draino. Your clothes for example,
where do you get the dye? Shoes, the adhesives. Drycleaners. What do you do
with that by-product? Jewelry, everybody likes a nice ring and a watch. But
there's going to be a by-product. Same thing with food. At large quantities, it's
going to be hazardous. Walmart, Target, Lowes, tons of damaged goods. We
take care of that. The worst was the Pierre Cardin. Week after week it kept
coming, acrid sweet smell. Bad-run on cologne, head starts pounding. All of
us took notes. Shooting-range bullets—lead bullets, excavate the bullets or
there's going to be environmental damage. Particulate matter. We take care of
that. What we have is a legacy issue. Stock-piles all over the world. Nerve-gas
disposal. To be a world power, you have to have something defensible. You
don't want to admit it. By truck and by rail. Flammable, poisonous, corrosives,
liquids, sludges, solids. We asked if he ever saw anything like poetry. He
leaned out of his seat, grabbed a bucket. Dinosaur poop, he said, passed the
bucket around like a bread basket. We took our pieces, placed them on the
table. They formed a tiny Stonehenge there. We find fossils, he said. This is
inland prehistoric ocean. In the entry way, you'll see 13 Plesiosaurus vertebrae.
I like going down there into the excavation site and finding the fossils. Never
get any shark's teeth. The others do. Just last week, they found handfuls of
them, and I was just out there. Right there in that spot. Me? Nothing. He looked
down at his hands. And what of that fool's gold, that shit we'd arranged? Some
sort of monument? Temple? What sacrificed? Remains inscrutable.

BLACKBIRD YAWNS IN THE HAZARDOUS WASTE

Chem Waste; Emelle, Alabama—largest hazardous waste site in the U.S.

I

Among 2700 acres
only 640 acres
are filled with microencapsulation, macroencapsulation, and direct landfill.

II

I was mindful of my mindlessness
like a hazardous waste site
on which there is a Certified Wildlife Habitat.

III

The safety manager explained the procedures.
We don't want anybody getting hurt here.

IV

A full medical check-up
every other year.
A pulmonary check
every year.

V

I had not known the word
decon
a decon building
a decon room
in every building.

VI

A horse trailer hung from the ceiling
in the PCB Barn, signs
of the waste scrubbed
into signs of the hazard
Notice, Hot Zone, Danger
Moving Caution Moving Parts

VII

How many of you know
about the Hudson River Project?
How many of you have heard
about Anniston, you know,
here in Alabama?

VIII

I am silenced by the super sacks
and tote trucks, and 5 million gallons of leachate,
but I know too
that my silence is involved
in the hazardous waste.

IX

We have our own ambulance,
our own fire-truck
our own EMT,
if anything should happen,
it's so far out here.

X

At trench 22, red clay sludges
from a truck driven by a black operator,
anyone of us in our van
may have been yawning.

XI

The operator stepped out
of his cab, down onto the site.
See, see how he has on
his full protective gear?
See his gear?

XII

The exothermic reaction is misting.
The hazardous waste must be rising.

XIII

It was as far as you could see.
It was a containment.
And it was an attempt to contain.
The hazardous waste lies
on Selma Chalk.

THE LAND OF K

There is a K inside you.

It is the land of K. K public housing. K public classrooms. K privatized incarcerations. K birds the cuckoo, every kind of cuckoo calling *cuckoo cuckoo cuckoo*, and the yellowhammer wood *peck peck peck* pecker.

K is a folk fiction, you proclaim, and I too like to think of the crisp white caps of K covered by watery acres, rock thick as the Lincoln monument sunk as killock, case closed. Yet, K continents cleave together cleave adrift, excitements commence increase collapse extinct, new cloisters configure crescents circle, tides roll *kshhhh kshhhh kshhhh*.

Everyday, in the land of K, the schoolbus quits the kids back from killjoy, they cross the crosswalk blinkers *click* door *click* octagon light smacks back *click*, skilled as caught daylight, a kid carries on clips along *skip skip skip*.

He skitters across to become a skit in the K park. Kid his own K his kingdom of kidcraft and kicks. Look! Okay? Cop on, he's a-okay? Ok, no questions, he's got a jacket, in his pockets the candy caught holding the whole kit-and-kaboodle, right here on MLK! Before any can counter or quarrel, the K dream inside you is taking effects. That K is like gold, like collateral.

II. HOW CONSUMING

And every stare can feather
in sudden throngs of pain

BLACKBIRD IDENTIFIES A CONCERTED EFFORT

*Alabama Coastal Bird Fest 2014, Excursion #207—Bottle Creek Mound Island
   Adventure*

I

Along the Tensaw River,
The first bird identified
Was a plastic owl.

II

I was without a signal,
Like sturgeon waters
In which sturgeon no longer exist.

III

It's a Samsung.
I like it cuz it's cheaper than an iPhone. *cheep cheep*

IV

Epicenter of trade. Creek Indians. Redneck Rivera. Great Blue Heron (*flying*,
   7:56 a.m.)

V

Kingfisher (*perched*, 7:59 a.m.)
I see 'im.
I do too!
Plastic bottle (*floating*, 8:11 a.m.)
Plastic bottle (*floating*, 8:13 a.m.)

VI

Glug-glug-glug spilled the morning
with the Osprey's engine.
180,000 acres owned by the state.
2nd largest natural
gas reserves.
Styrofoam cup (*floating*, 8:18 a.m.)

VII

Why is it that
She goes everywhere birding,
she's been all over the world—
We make a concerted effort
to see this odd bird—
we have to complete our list—
We have to is consuming?

VIII

Great blue heron (*flying*, 8:26 a.m.)
Great egret (*perched*, 8:27 a.m.)
Great blue heron (*flying*, 8:28 a.m.)
What happened?
Aw, aw . . . (*splashing*, 8:30 a.m.)
Great egret (*flying*, 8:31 a.m.)
Plastic marker (*tied*, 8:31 a.m.)
What do ya'll see?
I'm just taking pictures of the lichen on the log.
Lichen (*lichening*, 8:33 a.m.)
Plastic marker (*tied*, 8:34 a.m.)
Great blue heron (*flying*, 8:35 a.m.)
Great egret (*flying*, 8:41 a.m.)

IX

When the Native Americans paddled down all the way from Montgomery,
Alabama, and they made this turn right here, at Bottle Creek. *glug-glug-glug*

X

People always ask
if this is the island. There's no gift shop.
It's not very Disneyesque.
Oooo they're Indian spirits
in there. They say come in here
and we'll scalp ya!

XI

Saw Palmetto and insect *eeeeeee*

Step on stick, *T & eeeeeee*

This is Mound A. We actually passed through several of the mounds but you'd never know it. With ground-sensing sonar, they found bumps . . . it was artifacts . . . people lived there, that's how they knew where to dig. *eeeeeeeee*

Little brown newt (*hiding*, 9:14 a.m.) *eeeeeeee*

Plastic marker (*tied*, 9:15 a.m.) *eeeeeeee*

eeeeeeee Plastic marker (*tied*, 9:16 a.m.) *eeeeeeee*

Little brown newt (*captured*, 9:26 a.m.) + five cameras—two zooms, one flash

It's like Tarzan, *Ah-aaaahah!*

Well, I don't know the name of this right here.

It's grape vine.

Personally, I like it like this, untouched. *eeeeeeee*

XII

Men: 12

Women: 14

People of Color: 0

XIII

glug-glug-glug

In our wake (*fleeing*)

Great egret (*flying*, 10:29 a.m)

Turtle (*diving*, 10:30 a.m.)

Turtle (*diving*, 10:37 a.m.)

Turtle (*diving*, 10:42 a.m.)

Turtle (*diving*, 10: 43 a.m.)

Unidentified white bird (*flying*, 10:48 a.m.)

Plastic marker (*tied*, 10:49 a.m.)

Plastic marker (*tied*, 10:50 a.m.)

Aluminum can (*floating*, 10:50 a.m.)

There's a reception tonight.

What are we eating, fried chicken? [laughter] *glug-glug-glug*

Fish? (*leaping*, 10:52 a.m.)

Kingfisher, belted kingfisher (*flying*, 10:58 a.m.)

glug-glug-glug

Plastic bottle (*floating*, 10:59 a.m.)
Plastic bottle (*floating*, 11:00 a.m.)
glug-glug-glug
White man with dogs in speedboat (*smiling, waving, passing,* 11:01 a.m.)
glug-glug-glug
glug-glug
glug
gl-
ug-

WWW.HUMMER.COM

👍 the smallest of all
birds with our largest of all

SUVs [www.we.too.can.travel.to.the.ends.of.
the.earth.net] [www.we.too.are.

some.of.the.most.versatile.net] [www.
distinctly.unique.most capable.net] [www.

thousands.of.possible.configurations.net] [www.you.
never.dreamed.possible.net] [www.if.you.are.

a.hummer.you.are.a.perfect.balance.a.double.
take.wherever.you.re.headed.net] [www.

an.integral.part.of.our.DNA.net] [www.100.percent.
HUMMER.net][www.they.are.

no.longer.being.net]
[www.they.are.driven.net]

[ON BIRD BANDING]

Alabama Coastal Bird Fest 2014, Excursion #401—Fort Morgan

[I

[Fr[][] j[]w[]lry for birds, brac[]l[][]t bangl[]
        clos[] bosom-fri[]nd of th[] hand-cuffs;
conspiring with th[]m how to manag[] the riotous
        with aluminum, with stainl[]ss st[][]l,
with butt-[]nd bands, with lock-on & riv[]t bands,
        a round band with two []dges, a band
with two flang[]s of m[]tal, a band with flang[]s
        sid[]-by-sid[], a riv[]t lock[]d into plac[],
a band us[]d on birds that liv[] for many y[]ars,
        or birds that liv[] in salt-wat[]r
environm[]nts, bands for hawks and owls,
        bands for []agl[]s, a band that can b[]
r[]mov[]d by the bird[]r, but not by the bird.]

II

[Wh[]r[] []ls[] can you g[]t fr[][] j[]w[]lry for birds?
        Oth[]r in h[]r[], caught in th[] mist n[]t,
Wood Thrush, Thrash[]r, T[]nn[]ss[] [] Warbl[]r,
        y[]llow-b[]lli[]d Warbl[]r, Ruby-throat[]d Humm[]r,
bagg[]d h[]ad, fac[], fact and flit of you, hung
        from a hook, frantic a fir[] around which
th[] childr[]n wond[]r. What m[]asur[]m[]nts w[] go to
        for study of mov[]m[]nt patt[]rns, []stimat[]
of survival rat[]s, harv[]st pr[]ssures, to allow larg[]-scal[]
        analys[]s both spatially and t[]mporally, soft body
lift[]d among th[] instrum[]nts, on your back, spr[]ad
        thos[] l[]gs, rais[] thos[] wings up ov[]r your h[]ad, whil[]
w[] blow on your b[]lly. It's a pr[]tty one.]

III

[Who hasn't l[]t on[] go? Who wants to?
        Who can h[]lp it? W[] hold out our hands in
d[]for[]station, in som[] ar[]as larg[] for[]sts no long[]r
        []xist, to mak[] way for coff[][], to mak[] way
for cattl[], for mor[] disturbanc[]s of grassland ar[]as, mor[]
        roads, mor[] traffic, housing, and []v[]n dogs;
littl[] spac[], th[]s[] ch[]micals ar[] still us[]d;
        f[]w[]r plac[]s for n[]sting, f[]w[]r ins[]cts,
mor[] wind turbin[]s, mor[] n[]tt[]d and s[]rv[]d as d[]licacy,
        mor[] drought, fr[][]zing t[]mp[]ratur[]s, and so forth,
mor[] skyscrap[]rs in cities along migration
        paths; whil[] at night, mor[] mark[]d birds us[] the stars
to navigat[], and th[] gath[]ring numb[]rs soar in th[] s[]rv[]rs.]]

#IT'SGOINGTOBEOKAY

Alabama Coastal Bird Fest 2014, Excursion #401—Fort Morgan
For Ali

our birders catch a bird
& #bagthebody #isinflits
& the girl #Aspergers
leans down to it & coos
#it'sgoingtobeokay

#it'sgoingtobeokay since a very long time,
the news keeps coming so much
for the news #decliningnumbers
#watershortage #climatechange
so rarely that #it'sgoingtobeokay
it falls over us like a net that we deny
that we cannot deny but everyone hopes

#it'sgoingtobeokay
#everythinghappensforareason
#it'sallpartoftheplan
#scienceisalwaysfindingnewanswers
#it'sgoingtobeokay

we've got it in the bag
#woodthrush
#floor-dwellingbird
#songlikeaflute #song

👍 #it'sgoingtobeokay
#150millionyears
#fromoutofthedeepwoods
#hasrisenup&up&

#willfallsilent #the kingdom
#is #ourhands—

#THINGSTOSAVE

]#$$$ave the whales! well, oy wail ≈ #90%ofthebigfi$$$hgone ≈
that old $$$tati$$$tic ≈ #$$$avethe$$$tati$$$tic$$$f®omthem$$$elve$$$ ≈
they know not what they undo ≈ #$$$avetheMona®¢h$$$--
mete® of butte®flie$$$ ≈ #bee$$$ ≈ #bi®d$$$ ≈ #wo®d$$$mig®ating

totheothe®$$$ide ≈ www.i.have.$$$een.the.bea$$$t.mind$$$.net ≈
the gene®ation ≈ go on #$$$ale ≈ yet no $$$aving ≈ not even
ou®$$$elve$$$ ≈ [www.folk$$$y$$$entimentality.net]≈ [www.g®itty
®eali$$$m.net] ≈ $$$ave the g®een$$$ ≈ the $$$eizing ®ope$$$

to hang the wa® ¢®iminal$$$ ≈ #$$$avethewa®¢®iminal$$$ ≈ we'®e
banking on a wa® on wa® ≈ [www.¢an.you.$$$ave fo® pea¢e.net]
[www.pea¢e.is.fo®.giving.away.net] ≈ pie¢e by pie¢e ≈ lette®
by lette® ≈ [www.so.many.bodie$$$.laun¢hed.on.the.a®m$$$.of.our.fu®the®.
    net] ≈

#giveawaymyb®ide$$$ ≈ #myb®okena®t$$$ ≈
    #f®amethedeath$$$ofmyhea®t ≈
#no$$$avio® ≈ #nothingcanbe$$$aved [www.nothing
    $$$avewhe®ewe'®egoing.net][

LITANY OF THE AIN'TS

#Drymarchon
      ≈ there's merchant in us ≈
#Corais
      ≈it's 'Mercuh in us ≈
#Drymarchon
      ≈ fear's mercury in us ≈
#Coraishereus
#Corais
      ≈ surreptitiously
                near us ≈
#Body
      ≈ the Other in Heathen, *house serpent* in us ≈

[www.maintaining.corridors.is.important.net]

#Bodytheshunned ≈ reptile in the wood ≈
#Bodythelowly host
#LowlyvicinityhomeSod

[www.what's.served.is.to.spend.in.us.net]

#LowlyMouse
      ≈ *prey fear us* ≈
#LowlyMouseofSod
#LowlySnailofFreshwaters
Ain't Alabama Cave Fish
Ain't Paint Rock River Mussel
Ain't Gulf Sturgeon

[www.maintaining.corridors.is.important.net]

All ya'll lowly Albamahas and archalbamahas ≈
All ya'll lowly acres of extirpated and threatened species ≈
Ain't Alabama Beach Mouse
Ain't Blue Shiner
All ya'll lowly flora and fauna ≈

Ain't Red Hills Salamander
Ain't Endemic Dark Pigtoe
Ain't Heavy Pigtoe

[www.maintaining.corridors.is.important.net]

Ain't Shiny-rayed Pocketbook
Ain't Shiny Pigtoe
Ain't White Wartyback
Ain't Alabama Lampmussel
Ain't Pink Mucket
Ain't Finerayed Pigtoe
Ain't Tulatoma Snail
Ain't Slender Campeloma, giving birth to live snails
All ya'll lowly snails & anthropods & amphibians
All ya'll lowly inhabitants w/ the Drymarchon
All ya'll lowly rarities
All ya'll lowly mammals

[www.maintaining.corridors.is.important.net]

Ain't Grey Wolf
Ain't Humpback
Ain't Bluewhale
Ain't Florida Panther
All ya'll 180 mussel species
    $\approx$ 60 percent of the nation's mussels $\approx$
All ya'll freshwater streams
All ya'll lowly mammals
All ya'll lowly fishes & anthropods

#the[un]sharesofthedollar
From the spirit of fun-ication
#morethan4,000 caves
#temperateclimatesbesthopeforplantdiversity $\approx$
#Alabahmaaclimatepreciselythat $\approx$
#77,000milesofrivers&streams

#563,000acresoflakespondsandreservoirs&3millionacresofsweet-watermarshes ≈
#deltas&50milesofcoast
#containingnotonlysaltmarshesbut400,000acresofestuaries
#onceshallowpre-Cambriansea
#PineadmirableAscension

[www.maintaining.corridors.is.important.net]

#hereus
#woodsclearcut
#woodsparkinglots
#woodsdrilledwith2ndlargestproducerofnaturalgas
#woodsmountain-topremoval
#woodsWasteManagementInc
         ≈ largest hazardous waste site in the US ≈
woodsSuperfunds
#AnnistonPCBSite
#AnnistonArmyDepot
#CapitolCityPlume
#woodstocyanidearseniccadiumchroniumcopperleadnickelzinc
#bringbacktheTombigbeeRiverandfreshwaterwetlands
#periodicflooding
#locatednearseveralformerdisposalareas
#woodContaminantsofconcern
#DDT
#DDT-related products (DDTR)DDD&DDE
#hexachlorocyclohexane(BHC)isomersalphabetadelta &gamma BHC
   &chlorobenzene
#woodscleanupmetals
#semivolatileorganics
#volatileorganics&polyaromatichydrocarbons
#suchaslead
#suchaschromium
#suchasselenium
#suchasstyrene
#acrylonitrile
#phenol

#woodsrenderinfernallessenings

[www.maintaining.corridors.is.important.net]

#allbowerbreathingflockingshores
#woodshowenlivenbowershoals
#landtheshoalsofourbreathingrivers
#breathingflockingshores
#infernallessening
#liveandswervetheloopsservetheswerve
#ramble&bramble
#ya'lltoallthefruitydepartures
#America.sAmazon
#racinglynearus
#thenerveofus

[www.maintaining.corridors.is.important.net]

#ShunnedofSod
   weeds racingly stitch to worlds, nerve of us

#LimbofSod
   who snakest a way for the two minds of the world
      floor us, low's lore

#LimbofSod
   who snakest a way under to over lore
      as lush hush here us
#SlipofTongue
   how snakest a way
      heaving sea to scene in us
   long-quickening, rivercasting Sod
   may we maintain you & sow moved
#flashmadeflesh
#weedyneedlestitchingdark2lightdeath2lifeash2as
#DrymarchonColuberCorais

#Reptilegenus
#reptilegenius
#raptwildgenes-N-us
#rraptrrrrr....rrrr&s s s

```
            s s s s        s
              ss
              s  S  s s          s
                      s  s
                     ss
          s  s
          s
            S
              s
                s  s s&
                      s
                       s  s
                        s
                      s
                  s  s
               ss
          s
        S  &
            s
              s
                s  s s
                    & s
                  s  s
                          sss            SsS

                                    s        s
                                              &
```

ALL WHO WALK

What lands lord the riverwalk? what in the lord is this lands all who walk? what when lord verb to walk the riverwalk to lord? what is lord over? what is lord under? a host of knobby riverwalk river cooters lords while neon nylon shorts *thump thump thump* the trail's heartbeats or is beaten the fog wafts the deodrant wafts and as a barge of coal laden back slips along the Black Warrior river walk's, water glinting with carcinogenic yet youthful highlights. who among us are not the twins pushed along as the river walk two young pigeons or a pair of turtles to be offered? what lord the river walk 300 miles from top to bottom? what who lord over? what who lord under? What who how lore river walk the River State? what who how lore river walk 27 freshwater fish species (4 federally listed as endangered) 36 species of mussels (5 federally listed as endangered) 15 turtle species (1 federally listed as threatened) an endangered snail. the endangered snail is a riverwalk in which the lord sits in the withered hand of the weather.

THE FISHERMAN
Gulf Shores Pier

One must not have a mind of water
to read the signs #ShiftingShores
#StrugglingtoSurvive #GonewiththeWind

nor let loose your line,
to stop & listen [www.it.s.like.my.own
little.aquarium.net] [www.can.we.go.to.the.beach.

now.net]—and be human, not
#AlabamaBeachMice
#development #storms #foot traffic

not #ADiversityofLife
#OurGulfWatersTeemingwithLife
#TreasuresfromtheGulf

For [www.I.m.not.getting.any.fish.Daddy.net]
[www.Why.am.I.not.net]
[www.Why.am.I.not.net]

HOPE

Hope is a subtle glutton, and that's how hope Chase Adcox had a vision at 13 years of age to develop hope country club golf course becomes mixed family use housing units. The crowd's roar rolls across the acres. The acres pour into concrete slab with two-car garage. And that's really his name, hope Chase Adcox, chasing adding cocks as the hope river cooters—*deeper, deeper, don't stop!* Does every morning his tousled blond hair his cocking popping out of his boxers so much like those hope river cooters turtle heads cocks popping from this soon-to-be unponded pond. Now hope Chase Adcox owns himself an orgy of hope river cooters hope Chase Adcox's peek-a-boo. Is it porn impulse or commitment that draws my family down to the water for our daily morning's welcoming. Then, when we see it's not your hand in your pocket pond but that you're glad to see me, our hearts fill with hope a shield around me, my glory, the One and Many who lifts my head high. And now, hope Chase Adcox, how you own these acres and all they do trademarked such that my spirit rises in my chest is your hope Chase Adcox popping cocking. This is a grim vision.

I lie down on the grass sprayed with only hope Chase Adcox knows what. Me and them there your hope river cooters we hope enjoy basking in the sun on logs or rocks, but are quick to take to the water in the slightest threat of danger. How we feel ourselves stir and now that that stirring yours and so we are a threat to ourselves. We leap into the murk of you/me/us hope Chase Adcox. That's where we are now. Thousands of gallons of pond water and algae pressing in filling our lungs our ears our noses our dark open cunts. It's impossible to close ourselves to hope Chase Adcox, you too inside you too a popping cocking—yet, in the dark, it's clear that that hope is grope is the thug with fathers. Inside here in the muck, our hope is the ring with features, crowning. Can you feel the quickening tearing here stretching? Something's happening inside you. I pronounce it in the flames of the water, the sun, and the lowly spirits. They're in you, your crowning achievement. Waters breaking. Heads crowning. Once seized by those little faces so like your face, your very owned face hope Chase Adcox, you'll be for rivers changed. How consuming is love and hope is a subtle glutton.

#SINGSAME®ICA™

Snowy Plover Nesting Site, July 4, 2015—Gulf Shores, AL

#singsAme®ica™

#SnowyPlove®
We dig up the dunes by the wate®
When the bank$$$ come
So he®e™ ci®cles
And sta®ves
And g®ows fewe®

Tomo®®ow™
He®e™'ll be a me®e fable
When the child®en come
Nobody'll smile
Say to us
Look in the dunes
Then™

Today™
We see how beautiful™ he®e™ is
& [www.we.keep.going.net]

#singsAme®ica™

EME®ALD COA$T™

Seaside, Florida

The water is clear today™
The waves calm ever so soften, the sun sleeking
foam florescent
boards the ° children flaunt ≅ inflatable floats lift ≅ drift
bodies ≅ wet in our clutched cradles ≅ a sweet lull ≅ bought ≅
Look! #It.sajelly-fish! #GetitonyourGoPro!
playlist ≅ chirrup of text © jangle
of ice-cream truck ⓘ everywhere
is ° anywhere is #amusement™ ≅
underneath the tug
of undoing and its infinite indifference ∞
　°

Lucretius sensed °
somethings in the err ≈ a hunger's
thousand seraphs °swerving into terrific ≈
chancing on the deeds of the needless ≈
ruining around like a plunge of heedless
quickens ≈ a reel bundle of curves ≈ total
bacterias ° ≈ suns of the pitched ≈ °
°

Natural Balance™ is
ground mete ≈ once a perfect ° harmony
the tones of a ° major chord progression ≈ Instead ≈
now I hear clam °r °us ≈ pointless ≈ leaping noise ≈
Wholly unmodern ≈ unbroken ≈ some gallumphing
heart at the heat of things ≈ sings
say ≈ un ≈ say ≈ dawn say ≈ scene ≈ it's from beflower ≈
　°

° ≈ how we love™ to lie
here ≈ taking it easy ≈ while the earth unruly
churns its urns ≈ undertaking
the various b°untiful anew ≈ waking
all's night ≈ has #~~bigfish~~ #~~bigcat~~
#~~bearelephantsongbirdbutterflybee~~
& here we are on a blinding plain ≈
dashed *buy°buy* delirium and delight ≈
paradise the world over in our sites[1]

---

[1] www. ∞™.net

III. OF THE UNDERSTORY

"Love it Leave it Love it Leave it Love it Love it Leave it Love it"

And we all shine on.

YELP

Guntersville State Park

this st△te p△rk is v△st with beloved ≈ th△t high wooded ridge
e△ch d△y △ l△ke-view ch△let she swings-n-the-h△mmock ≈
u'll he△r how being △*△*△*△ = overlooking ≈
over ≈ how it's looking ≈ extensive L△ke Guntersville
Tennesse△n river downwind from the nucle△r pl△nt
torn △do's s△plings slower th△n clim△te △greement ≈

△ △   △
△ △

△ 9 ≈ bec△use she w△nts to s△ve the △m△zon ≈ be
life ≈ lovely l△ke ≈ blue herons ≈ flock-n-flight ≈ geese goslings ≈
she'll look 4 cre△tures ≈ come b△ck △rmed to the se△s with tr△sh ≈
find △ mess△ge-n-△-bottle ≈ C△den Potts wuz here ≈
u & ur beloved c△n both reply ≈ write letters
to the future ≈ toss ur words to the w△ters ≈ too find
next mess△ge ≈ PS: I h△ve △ secret butt-cr△ck st△sh ≈

YELP

Lodge Trail, Guntersville Lake State Park

ξ

  ξ

ξ

ξ

I havξ to rξlivξ a fξw hξat rails about this trail

    On thξ map in thξ mom ≈ this trail is clξarly markξd shout

Why doξs the bξlovξd ask u not to talk so much

    about snakξs whξn clξarly u R thξ map, and that's why!

u'rξ s/mothξring is a bad trail with no bξginning

    nor ξnd no friξnd only fiξnd fiξ foξ, *wahhhhh* in the trξξs....

     ξ

   ξ

  ξ

ξ

If thξrξ's fun thing I lξarnξd from Taylor mountain it's this:

    Smothξr and doubtξr is nothing orangξ shξrbξrt can't fix,

Excξpt accξpt now u must goad buck up thξ mountain...

    thξ April 27th tornado & now u:

I'm thξ map! My world missus! No morξ Supξr Bubblξ!

    At thξ top, thξ bξlovξd jokξs, thξ farcξ is wit's duξ.

I suggξstξd thξy rξnamξ thξ trail Dξarth Mothξr

 ξ

   ξ

  ξ

YELP
DeSoto State Park

⌘

       ⌘

   ⌘

Stayed fær three nights gæing sæuth after Mæuntain Wærkshæp
     We arrived æn the ræcks ≈ trickled alæng the Little ≈
lææked æut ≈ signed up w/ the millipedary ≈

         ⌘

            ⌘

          ⌘

    ⌘

Upæn return gæt ticked æff ≈ sæmeæne stæle my stick
Sæ bælted dæær ≈ Lit an indæær fire ≈ Smæke chæked ≈ staked
æut æn pærch ≈ næ ☺ with serrated knife was æbserved ≈
Cæuld næt sleep ≈ Held vigil ≈ Gæt up ≈ Tææk shæwer ≈ Fæund græin tick ≈
Plucked with knife tweezers/bræke æff gæddamn head ≈ Bellæwed ≈ Swære ≈
Child afeared with me bleared with tick ≈ ticked untæ Fært Payne ≈

           ⌘

         ⌘

       ⌘

       ⌘

          ⌘

       ⌘

Never færget hæw we babbled alæng the river ≈
Catawaba cascade fireside raccææns blue ghæst
fireflies azaleas aræse ææææ's penned sky ≈ We camped
at DeSætæ State Park in a rhædædendræn blææm

      ⌘

    ⌘

     ⌘

     ⌘

       ⌘

     ⌘

A**A*A*A OF THE DEER TICK

      o

                     oo

          o

              o

        o

When he ch°°ses u as his succulent ≈ digs u
       talks ab°ut n°thing but yr azalea cascade hike
°f the groin yrs ≈ that u R s° swell ≈ h°w he whispered
              o

what ♥ ≈ Delici°us ♥ in yr lap lapping u up
       that ♥er °f crevices a seeker °f yr heat
lust wanted t° get inside y°u bl°°d this treasure °f his
            o

       o

         o

he's the s°rt °f thug wheedling t° get in yr jeans
       vamping secreting scheming seams seams his everything
wh° slips int° bed ≈ u n°w wedl°cked t° this thick nit
           oo

       o

          o

        o

  o

then pulled fr°m u flailing newb°rn at the tit ≈ drunken
       pathetic at the tap ≈ h°w u kicked him t° the fl°°r,
h°w c°uld u kn°w he'd break apart? h°w he l°st his head ≈
       h°w sucked yr luck n°w stuck bearing his b°rrelia
         o

               oo

       o

  o

A**A*A*A OF THE MYCILIEUM

<pre>
                ii   i
            i i   i
        ¡'ve spent my one m¡ld l¡fe hunt¡ng for w¡ld morals ≈
bod¡es g¡v¡ng egg and volva asway ≈ that flyway ¡ ¡ ii   ¡ ii   ¡
¡   ¡ ¡
        they bear hear beneath the sound of these veering feet
                            ¡ ¡   ii   ¡ ii   ¡
                            ¡ ¡
of spores ¡f each of one puffball became a morel
¡ ¡   ii   ¡ of the understory ≈ how the fru¡t¡ng bod¡es could
c¡rcle our earth w¡th a netted sk¡rt more a mature
            ¡ ¡   ¡
                      ¡
        st¡nkhorn lack¡ng a sk¡rt ≈ look ≈ v¡xen parasol ≈
¡ ¡   mut¡nus phallus ≈ st¡nkhorn ≈ swell¡ng thrum hear dear reader ≈ ¡   ¡
you stalked me walked ground around small manners ≈ fru¡t body¡¡   ¡
                        ¡   ii   ¡ ¡
            ¡   ¡   ¡ ¡   ¡
sputter¡ng m¡n¡ature mutter¡ngs ≈ bra¡n l¡ke a sponge
¡ ¡   loam foams mag¡c too made s¡ck sod's bra¡n stem ≈ what sod ¡s
th¡nking g¡ft to badgers ≈ deer ≈ m¡ce ≈ p¡gs ≈ rabb¡ts ≈ squ¡rrels
        you fly lover ≈ land¡ng on the sl¡me ≈ gobbl¡ng l¡t up
            iii
                ¡ ¡
                                    ¡
</pre>

A**A*A*A OF THE TURKEY BUZZARD

>>>

>>>

to b>>> in th>>> cabin at th>>> >>>nd of R visit
of packing th>>> Things th>>> hammock th>>> bik>>> of wildhood
& th>>> scoot>>>rs & toothpast>>> of R co>>>xist>>>nc>>>

> >

>> >

> >>

> >>

tr>> luscious th>>> whol>>> vacay ≈ app>>>aringly >>>mpty
>>>xc>>>pt bow>>>rs th>>> minisculia of ins>>>cts
& th>>> g>>>n>>>raliti>>>s of foliag>>> ≈ four days &

th>>> last t>>>n minut>>>s ≈ Out-th>>>r>>>'s oak of awkward alights
pair of u that scruff tr>>>>>> scowl ≈ u'r>>> a Volt ≈ two with raw
of r>>>d pat>>>s & th>>> tr>>>>>> as gnarl flap claw ≈ May this Volt

>> >

>> >

> >>

> >   >

mov>>> through m>>> ≈ l>>>t flight sm>>>ll m>>> list>>>n as carrion
carry on in m>>> ≈ this rid>>>s invisibl>>> curr>>>nt ≈
it's in h>>>r vulture ≈ s>>>ns>>> m>>> into th>>> scav>>>ng>>>d now ≈
my night's fruiting body ≈ th>>> scrappy b>>>nd of yr b>>>ak >

>

>

YELP

Rickwood Caverns State Park

             {}

             {}

This state park was extremely unslept. It's a f{}XXX
& A**A*A*A were the {}nly {}nes at number thirteen
s{} it was very tent = s{} flimsy what was that n{}ise

        {}

        {}{}

yet what stirs in u when u leave the bread {}ut f{}r f{}XXX?
what wreck wrack decapitating metal trashcan heads
all fright. N{} ☺ w/ a serrated knife was {}bserved.

    {}

  {} {}

      {}

        {}{}

The next biggest attracti{}n was watching water drip
F{}rming f{}rmati{}ns an inch 4 every hundred {}r s{} years
a. wet 250 milli{}n year {}ld cave
b. A**A*A*A {}n her sc{}{}ter in the spun light
c. Playing p{}ker by the campfire & writing &
d. Living in a w{}rld that is n{}t spent n{}r saving
e. We camped at Rickw{}{}d Caverns in a vulvic f{}ld

               {}

.

                  {}

       *

                  .

                  {}

                  *

A**A*A*A OF THE GRAY FOXXX

What's it lick to yip in these woods? Yip yip ≈ yap yap ≈ yelp
      Is there ☺ with a serrated knife to be observed?

Are you more wolf ≈ dog ≈ deer's fear ≈ hey is there a cat for that?

      Hey there foXXXy shady? O fur foXXX staked, how do we
acres cleared in ur legends? I 👍 the lurk of you.
      Could you near us breathing? Death you thin want to meat us?

u booked w/ bread: Didn't 👍 the tomato we sent?
      Were the ticks in our tent ur reply? If trees grow
in soil with specific fungus ≈ if taxoplasmosis

      drives infected people to want more cats ≈ if these ticks
bit me bit you ≈ if u share me yours ≈ i'll share u mine ≈
      if bacteria ≈ if virus ≈ if protozoa ≈

w/ this bit I thee wed & the two shall be biome

A**A*A*A OF THE BESS BEETLE

                                        t

                                    t

            t t
I wish more of my days slow danced hand on the butt with
rotting logs in forests ≈ my mandibles their rivers ≈
O anthropod who art invertebrate ≈ o robust

                              t t t

                              t t t

                              t

bookish bug ≈ quiet ≈ what sort of library R u?
My antennae extinct species come black as a nightdress
My elytra deeply grooved by years spent backpacking

                                      t

                                      t

        t
thru fear's lips ≈ It's more sometimes I wish this antennae
were curved when relaxed ≈ u know? Bess, we log u so mulch!
Some days god gets so sky and flighty flit in the trees ≈ t

                                  t

Later days ≈ ground has undergown a constellation ≈
gathers caves ≈ sod's flow in humus shelf like a past's new fate
gods sleep wed to the world & u R officiant;
tree is beetle ≈ Beetle is tree ≈ that fall we kneel to

                    t

            t

            t

YELP

Cheaha State Park

∧typic∧l kid ∧nd me were ∧ble to ∧rgue
∧ lot here. While B∧throom ☺ bl∧sted "Dust in the Wind,"

we were close to Che∧h∧ Wilderness ∧nd be-
coming scene of ∧ veg∧n preteen run∧w∧y, so

there w∧s ∧ f∧ir ∧mount of ∧nnoyed from the R∧ven

C∧mpsite, No. 56. With our c∧mpfire t∧lks though, we kept the ∧nnoyed
from bitchy too much of ∧ new st∧nce. The primitive
sites rowed d∧rkness, shown we were sown moved to move

∧gainst her recent hurts, dr∧w d∧wn our powers know the st∧rs
could be breathing out the night, mount∧in flowing support

overhe∧d limbs torsos stretching in ∧ccord, nodding
off with my m∧ce in my h∧nd, whistle ∧t the re∧dy;

We c∧mped ∧t Che∧h∧ St∧te P∧rk in ∧n open door

A**A*A*A OF THE ANIMAL

XXX   XXX
       XXX
   XXX XXX

PrXXXy ≈ Untitled (FemXXXle Bust) ≈ and Untitled (MXXXle Bust)[2]
wXXXlk into the pXXXrk ≈ Other sXXXys to the one ≈ "Just how
do we get XXX think in here? R we supposed to be
     XXX XXX XXX
  XXX
    XXX

behind beXXXrs ≈ just us ruining XXXround like XXX hunch of
liminXXXls? If we're here ≈ does thXXXt meXXXn we don't gnXXXw our
plXXXce ≈ cXXXn't wreck XXXgonized our owned fXXXce? WhXXXt is XXX
 stXXXte
      XXX
      XXX XXX

        XXX
      XXX
pXXXrk if not XXXll these sow XXXnd sows corrXXXlling XXXll weeds
hXXXve in commons?" They eXXXch lXXXke XXX drink from the wXXXter
mountXXXin ≈ Light pops on in XXXn RV ≈ XXX silhouette
      XXX
    XXX XXX
    XXX
   XXX
Of XXX mXXXn with XXX shotgun ≈ WhXXXt XXXnimXXXls buck up
XXXnd kick, bodies gunning down the roXXXd most trXXXvelled by
go-cXXXrts ≈ their hooves stinging out their hXXXrd hit fists knocking
I see XXXs they leXXXp into the brush ≈ white tXXXles lXXXshing ≈
   XXX
  XXX XXX
   XXX
  XXX

---

[2] "Pray," "Untitled (Female Bust)," & "Untitled (Male Bust)" wandered in from Kate Clark's
sculptures.

YELP

Fort Payne Cabin Historic Site, Trail of Tears National Historic Trail

$ $

$ $

$

Thi$ review is ba$ed on an afternoon $hop ≈ The $ite
i$ not an acre near the cute hi$toric downtown ≈
boa$ting an organic fair-trade coffee hou$e ≈ The $pot
You R invited to think of them a$ you follow
$

$ $

$ $

their path ≈ The $ite is free to the public ≈ It's the $hame
gold $tory ≈ there word$ coffer world$ of 'removal fort$'.
In the tree$ a bu$ine$$ $ign read$ ≈ Convenient Wa$h
Acro$$ the $treet another bu$ine$$ ≈ Fort Payne Finance
$ $

$

$

$ $

$

$

On the gate a padlock'$ brand defray$ claim$ ≈ Ma$ter
Who i$ $peaking and paying what with 'Benge Detachment'?
We walk in $ilent meditation 13 loot$ ≈
I$ it meditation or are we unju$t $talking?
Hope'$ mule ≈ A**A*A*A ≈ Mom ≈ when will we be Flemi$h?
$

$

YELP
Oak Mountain State Park

∞

    ∞ ∞   ∞∞∞∞∞

∞∞∞ ∞∞ ∞∞∞∞

      ∞∞∞∞ ∞∞

        ∞∞∞∞

This state park had grieving t∞ d∞ ≈ had l∞st its father
and this year, a friend with tw∞ small children t∞ raise ≈
signs warned ∞f the pit vipers ≈ c∞tt∞n m∞uth ≈ timber back ≈

∞∞∞ ∞∞ ∞∞ ∞∞∞∞

     ∞∞ ∞∞∞∞∞∞∞

     ∞∞∞∞ ∞∞

       ∞∞∞∞

The father had been l∞ng ill and l∞ng s∞me h∞w estranged ≈
the friend had been unreliable ≈ g∞ne d∞wn ∞n uppers ≈
which is why the park is here instead ∞f at funerals ≈ ∞

         ∞ ∞   ∞   ∞∞∞∞ ∞∞   ∞

     ∞

      ∞ ∞∞∞∞

           ∞

         ∞

At the petting farm, the p∞t belly pig g∞es insane ≈
w∞rriedly pacing the b∞rder between here and there ≈
better t∞ j∞in the church gr∞up gathered ar∞und kumquats ≈

∞ ∞ ∞∞ ∞

∞∞∞ ∞∞∞∞

     ∞∞∞∞ ∞∞

       ∞∞∞∞∞∞∞ ∞∞

The tree trunks thick as a ☺ 's arm stretch ∞ver ∞ur heads ≈
in autumn the ∞aks leaves rattle ≈ is that a warning?   ∞
We have n∞ ch∞ice but t∞ c∞me cl∞ser ≈ sleep under them ≈
In ∞ak Mountain Park ≈ we slept in a n∞t yet claimed h∞le ≈

              ∞∞∞∞ ∞∞   ∞∞∞∞∞∞   ∞

        ∞∞∞∞ ∞∞

    ∞

YELP
Gulf State Park

                                        ♩

                ♩ ♩

         ♩

Th♩s Alabama State Park has Show Mouse Through Condos ≈
Homer the Gulf Box Turtle Attacker of Croc Shoes ≈
Left♩e the All♩gator One Who Doesn't Appear ≈

    ♩ ♩♩ ♩

                ♩ ♩

M♩dnight Cottonmouth Co♩led ♩n the Woods Beh♩nd the Tent
Merely A Plast♩c Wrapper Left by Former Tenants ≈
L♩ttle Green Frog Great Cr♩cket Trapped ♩n Bathhouse ≈ Shar♩ng

        ♩   ♩   ♩♩

              ♩♩

                ♩

the Beach Presentat♩on Protect♩ng Sea Turtle Nests ≈
Who ♩s protecting Ne♩l at the Front Desk ≈ How he wants
to wr♩te songs? Not Woman at Adventureland Redeems

        ♩   ♩

      ♩

T♩ckets Demand♩ng We Need the G♩ant Grabb♩ng Claw ≈
Who w♩ll w♩n the Adored Pr♩ze ≈ Amusement or Wonder?
No adventure ♩s replete w♩thout the fr♩sk of breath ≈
We slept at Gulf State Park ♩n Mom's one rema♩n♩ng lung

            ♩   ♩   ♩ ♩

                  ♩♩

              ♩

A**A*A*A OF THE FLORIDA SAND DOLLAR

✪

✪

Sometimes I thrash in to say please don't dick the waters ≈
get a bit cilia with this one girl collector ≈
she calls you her good cents ≈ she says she's just worked so hard
✪   ✪✪

to gather your far-fathom-sail-beyond-the-break-zone
     to turn you in for beach-combed-for-sale-at-local-shop ≈
Sometimes I stir & stir ≈ she stores & stores ≈ you go
✪   ✪   ✪

✪ ✪

pale as a smothering's loving hound pleases so-dulled
    people in deep brands ≈ sometimes I imagine that beached
one of you are streaming at the top of your tube feet ≈
✪   ✪

✪✪ ✪ ✪

I'm shot shore what to do, just how to glint her to sea
    the bounty of your flower mouth opens the center
of her hungering body ≈ how hand it to her ✪
    toss farther than her father's defiledest feverish schemes

✪

✪ ✪

IV. FRUITY DEPARTURES

By moonlight
We tossed our pebbles into the lake
And marveled
At the beauty of concentric sorrows.

BLACKBIRD SLIDES DOWN GIGNORMOUS TOILET SLIDE

Southern Environmental Center, Birmingham, Alabama

I

Among 20–30 homeschooling families,
The place where all the rivers lead
Was bright within each at the Southern Environmental Center.

II

I was mother to a swirling mass of all this trash
Like a classroom
In which the carpet is made of plastic bottles,
The insulation is recycled newspaper,
This floor is recycled cars, and
We're actually at the bottom of a swimming pool.

III

The Southern Environmental Center has lived all over the world.
It was making a mountain out of a garbage tsunami.

IV

A toilet and a cockroach
Are one.
A toilet and a cockroach and a trashcan
Are one: *Bloph!*

V

In the heart, there are two Alabamas—down
The hill privet, brambles, trash
Then there's this part
[Gestures to the Southern Environmental Center]
home of 8,000 abandoned urban lots, of Forbes 5th most dangerous city, of 7th for
year round particle pollution, 5th for short-term particle pollution, of largest
      hazardous waste site in the U.S., of 1st in the U.S. for the greatest amount
      of biodiversity is the Mobile-Tennesaw Delta, America's Amazon

VI

Brick from Bessmer paved the windy trail
With unnamed labor.
The voice of the Southern Environmental Center

A leave-no-trace approach, walk lightly.
The quarried granite spun on-toe:
The mastodon in the garden.

VII

Children in audience, how does it make you feel?
Energy vampires.
Why not instead plug for the Southern Environmental Center
At the kite-flying festival
In a fish costume?

VIII

I remember the 1970s
And the average of 2 pounds of trash per person per day;
But now I gnaw the news
Says the Southern Environmental Center,
It's 6.5 pounds.

IX

When the Southern Environmental Center said let's have some trash talk here,
We lived among the porous dirty as *weeeee*
Slid down gignormous toilet slide.

X

At the site of the Southern Environmental Center,
Moving is the trashopolis
The youngest among us thrilled:
No way! How does it do that? A second ball! A third ball!

XI

Later that day, I walked through walls
In my kitchen.
From that office, cheer lifted me
In that I filed the local bureau of my recycling bin
As the Southern Environmental Center.

XII

The storm drain is foxing.
The Southern Environmental Center must be natural kidneys.

XIII

It was all gonging song.
It was a ball and a chain.
It was a bell and change.
The Southern Environmental Center trills
Among the Trillium.

TOAD

A toad can die of light when Water, damn, see how when you hold her down, house's eyes light up! Inside house, a toad in a hole starting to chant a name from inside my body, a my song say my name toad in a hole singing love of a hole.

This toad is like a fat wet circled by a fatter wetter, and on the unscene side of the fatter wetter, arise choirs. Not all men all women boys girls flora fauna fowl fish deep sea amoeba choirs. My song say my name toad choirs none have heard, to songs making a write. Or rather, on the unscene side flickers silent my song say my name toad flicks. Not familes, comedies, nudities, or snuff. The flicks reel with something like at the birth, the blood flowing down my thighs and onto the floor, like poured down the drain flows out to the river to the sea. You must watch this watershed only from a distant rooftop but could say the white lights flash by like a child's wordless somersaults, weapons eager to destroy the army marching is my sentences.

Meanwhile, not my song say my name toad toad directly on the banks of rivers and creeks burrows throughout my body and this toad ash dust blowing off waste sites this toad 5.5 billion pounds of contaminated wastewater, this big toad bugged out toad trypophobia such that my holes fill with this toad 44 slurry lagoons. My song say my name toad croaking pretentious nonsense. My song say my name toad must either hold its breath and float or sink to the bottom toad punctured bladder, vapid and limp.

All day long, I'm toadily one who doesn't know she's two toads, a my song say my name toad toad tree frogs and allies and that toad trypophobia, all day long, I'm holding my breath. Everybody has to work. All day long, with everybody at work, my name leaks out from somewhere through the cackles in my *ribbet ribbet*'s, all day long, decomposing bacteria releasing methane under a frozen lake.

Someone steps out onto the lake. They have their cold weather clothing, are wearing crampons to keep from slipping, know how to read the ice. They've come to drill with an augur, to illuminate the lake. They've come to snap a photo. Please be careful, drilling someone, with your augur, a toad can die of light!

THE LIGHTHOUSE, THAT'S A GOOD TITLE
Oak Mountain Petting Zoo

#TodaywascompletelikeanAmerican Girl
    doll.sshirtpantshat #Yoursmileisbetterthan

achairattheendofalongday #There.s
    athingcalledtop-shelfliquor #You.dbethat

#Youtheoppositeofwhenmyheartsinks
    #SometimesIthinkGodisjust

adisappointedchemistactingout

    anaughtychildwithabigflashlight

whatascientistdoestoapigtonoapig
    #aporkothesis #aporktheosis #Idon.tknow #I know

you.renotthat #youmakermeamother #youwho
    noweachpigapal #yourpaltheologyappealing

#yououttherestaringintothefire #yourtotemanimals
    #thered-tailedhawk #themotorcycle

A**A*A*A OF THE GREAT I AM



A**A*A*A sleep in the cr ≈ drkness rustles us ≈
I'm getting up the tent in the eyes of the lights ≈
eyes winks the sky ≈ eyes blinks the woods ≈ eyes stinks open pores

When off to my side ≈ berd nd wide hir wild ≈
 ☺ is wtching me ≈ He's not wering  shirt ≈
Is it the ☺ with the serrted knife ≈ rptor prowl?

When he sees me fleeing him ≈ He sys ≈ "Um, didn't men
to scre you ≈ I sw you lover her and thought you
might could use um help ≈ Do you wnt um help?"

I flre ≈ & tht's when I relize the berd is burning
s do lives in some men's eyes ≈ yet his were not consumed ≈
the next morning ≈ I see him nd his husbnd drive by
clling from the berd ≈ & I wve ≈ & I sy ≈ *Here I m* ≈

FORBIDDEN

Forbidden fruit a flavor has for itself.

It has a bright green taste for its own itness, stretching out its bawdy body, it's bending over to touch its hills dipping its fingers into it the river on which it walks.

You tart! It says to itself, a smile wielding a belt.

Forbidden fruit invites forbidden trespassers to be prosecuted, persecuted, so cute is it?

Forbidden fruit's shaved frame dressed to keel its curves bared across sings the street.

The tears in its fishnet widen, the fish through the afternoon air swim right up to my window, waking I contracts in a flood plain.

The sound of their heads ramming on the glass, inside the sound of their skulls crushing is the 6th mass extinction.

The sensation of their heads rammed on the glass blood unvieling the air comes untendered through my window, swishes its fishy longing here, nibbles on the dead skin of my heart.

Forbidden fruit breaks open upon the rocks of our forbidden love, spilling warm innards across my desk.

The stench the wetness the deference is spreading.

In the tiny broke-open faces at my feet, I see them star and spar behind a fence, wearing out warring in aviary collars, each movement a tree in a conservation easement a ballerina's tattooed arms, undulant winged cherubs, someone else's name.

The forbidden fruit pines leans to dance for me and only me and for every passersby and only itself, ravenous knock out forbidden to possess a pistol.

Forbidden fruit of our love between us police on patrol and five hundred years of property law, fruit forbidden a bazooka, hand grenade, missile, or explosive or incendiary device; a pistol, rifle, or shotgun; or a switch-blade knife, gravity knife, stiletto, sword, or dagger; or any club, baton, billy, black-jack, bludgeon, or metal knuckle, all this split spilt spit upon bleeding forbidden fruit has is the forbidden joy of the godless, which in the end, will it be enough to make a new life?

Possessed by a pistol, the fruits of whose labor, the legacy of how now its stairs with wide open lies sterile as a golf course in the cursed of things, can it seed far enough into the development's furniture to seed forbidden fruit a flavor has for itself?

I FELL ASLEEP IN THE MIDDLE OF YOUR POEM, SORRY

Oak Mountain Campground

#Aboveustheusualstarspecks #Mercury #Venus #Mars #etc
#Aroundusthecampsitesspilledwithpeople #simple
camperstrail #squash #gourd #rootvegetables #plaintains

#Thewoodsatnight #twofemalebodiesfearyeyed
#tsunami'sviolence #ragingtornadoes #psychopathicrage
#oritthatjusttheriverburblingby #traffic.soceaniclull

#fromthespringthatistheindustrialrevolution? #Thetigerisendangered
#terrible #yetifthesewoodsweretigeriferous
#I.dwishthemverymuchtobecommondonkeyorgoat

#whichiswhywe.renotinthetent #sleepinginthecar
#Anythingcouldbeoutthere! #Evenanandroidwithamotorcycle
#Besidesit.scozyinhere #thedoorslocked #thesleepingbags #theflashlights

#snuggledup
#Justyou #me #DonaldTrump

CAN WE DO ANOTHER ONE?
Tannehill State Park

I want to loiter #herewithyou unfound
as a couple of oranges #highupinthebranches

of an orchard beside a #pioneercabininAtlantis. I want
to sing #cricketsallday #songwithyou hang by our tails

#yipcoyoteyap with you #crowsinthepines #in
thegrapes and consume #allthesunlightwarming

thecanopyinBrazil. I want to play #hooky
withyou, #feedthefish, shoulder #nothing #onthebeach

inIreland. I don't want to be #thebulletinyour
JFKparade, the #brokendreamonyourMLK, your #over

thathillmuseumofforgeries, I don't want our hearts to #grow
mold, go #heavywrongasaconfederatecannonball. No,

I want to be the #candyshelf.each.reflecting.jar. #Yourface
thesupplyroad. #Youreyesthesupplies. #Their smile. #Let'sstray[re]wild.

DEMONSTRATION CABIN
Tannehill State Park

My head has always been loud inside bride to everywhere streams glam with
fish-dash//let's dish out bread//we've dropped burnt cash from our mouths//
what is on the underside of the sign 'creek'? //Cross the plank bridge to see the
rebuilt forge ahead//for getting is the way to the slave quarters//what is on the
other side of *We had a wonderful hike in the woods*—did we bring lunch or will
we head back to the museum?//my head is the gift store, candy shelf I lick stick
slick sharpened tip, perfect for letting out sound openned//my head

bleeds onto the floor//the shopkeeper says no worries swept under a confederate
flag hat display for the kids, let's check out the mood rings, inside the stone
the burbling by buy blithey my heart this relocated pioneer cabin wares are
we? on the porch, who's the host of a quilting bee, visitors i almost recognize
bring news, a racing down a great white corridor to deliver us from what is still
born by the world//my heart the only mammal that flies trapped inside, robes
thrown back like

>   transparent wings
>   on a naked body, she dips
>
>   her lower jaws
>   into the world's wide wet
>
>   this beard
>   with leacheate
>   and lead
>   dripping

AZALEAS

Azaleas pink along the brick wall. Azaleas announcing another year has arrived.
When I look at the azaleas, I feel the azaleas inside me azaleas thinking home
bush. I put my head on azaleas thinking home bush and suckle suckle. I look
up into her azaleas wide open. Help me, Mommy! Help, me! Tell me it's all
going to be okay! Mommy smoking a cigarette and reading a fashion magazine.
Mommy star medallion lodged in my eye. Suckle suckle. H

er tears warm on my fontantel her nipples multiply like mushrooms my mouth
my lips pucker pinks that velvet. Pink's the suckle suckle milk fills my belly
and I drink from all the azaleas alive today and tomorrow is thrown from all
the azaleas flees like a shadow and does not remain all the azaleas so clothes the
grass in the field and feel and sow felled—Azaleas is my darling!

Yet, the day we are azaleas is my darling is the day we are azaleas highly toxic.
Because every day is highly toxic, I close mine eyes to the nukes of the world,
yet the nukes glow on the back of mine eyes where is writ the nukes that raze
nudes, that yes you rue know the rules: every day must be eaten. Every day
must be eaten before you may get up from the table. You will sit at this table
until you eat each and every day.

When you get up from the table, you go outside.

It is night. It has long been writ night is azaleas salivation, watering of eyes and
nose, abdominal pain, loss of energy, depression, nausea and vomiting, diarrhea,
weakness, difficult breathing, progressive paralysis of arms and legs, coma.
No matter. Every day will have been eaten. And night everywhere forthwith
wafts with pink azaleas swamp azaleas. Every day will have been eaten and
your plate clean as the night in which something moves, some low shadow
with a mind of its own, heart ripped from the tree, tree heart full of hop. It is
writ, you will give chase. You will run as far as the deer in the leaves departed,
further than the lost foundling. Run until you hold as your hands the wet
pulsing throb with a mind of its own in the azaleas is my darling in the azaleas
pink along the brick wall.

NOTES

The title A**A*A*A is a manifestation of *Albamaha*, the plural word for members of the Alabama tribe indigenous to the Mobile-Bay watershed.

The epigraphs sprout from Emily Dickinson; *Urban Tumbleweed: Notes from a Tanka Diary,* Harryette Mullen; *Deepstep Come Shining,* C.D. Wright; *A Murmuration of Starlings,* Jake Adam York, and *Twenty-Six Ways of Looking at a Blackman,* Robert Patterson, respectively.

"Dust Is The Only Secret" breathes research on the impact of coal dust from the article "Alabama's Blackbelt Region: A land forgotten, contaminated by coal ash," published on the Physicians for Social Responsibility website.

The "Blackbird" poems and "The Fishermen" are pollinated by the glistening hive Wallace Stevens; "The Land of K" is a fungal thread sent from the mother-tree Kim Hyesoon and is in memoriam to Tamir Rice and too many others, and owes a debt to the insights of Alina Stefanescu Coryell; "The Manager" is from a mold created after "The Colonel," by Carolyn Forché, was melted in an acid bath, poured, and let dry; "#singsAme®icaᵀᴹ" follows the chemical track that is Langston Hughes.

"Dust Is The Only Secret," "Azaleas," "Toad," "Hope Is A Subtle Glutton," "Forbidden A Flavor Has," wire-wrap first lines of Emily Dickinson's poems.

"Litany of the Ain'ts" sends a satellite signal to Endangered Animal Species of Alabama on the Encyclopedia of Alabama website and the Litany of the Saints.

The "Yelp" and "A**A*A*A of____" series were homegrown in a container garden as part of a grant supported project to travel to state parks throughout Alabama, titled "Emplaced and Multiple: Excursions in the Mobile-Bay Watershed for new poetic works."

"Demonstration Cabin" produced the chemical www.alabamapioneer.com, with many historical facts affecting plant growth, including that Birmingham Zoo and Botanical Gardens are built atop a mass grave of 4700+ poor Alabamians, mostly people of color.

"The Lighthouse, That's a Good Title," "I Fell Asleep in the Middle of Your Poem, Sorry," and "Can We Do Another One" were part of a capture and release program led by my daughter, Sophie Staples, using a collaborative procedure wherein she selected five categories and then filled those categories with words. The challenge then became to write a piece grounded in our current shared situation, teaching every word how to feed themselves.

ABOUT THE AUTHOR

HEIDI LYNN STAPLES' debut collection, *Guess Can Gallop,* was selected by Brenda Hillman as a winner of the New Issues Poetry Prize. She is author of three other collections, including *Noise Event* (Ahsahta, 2013), and her poetry has appeared in *American Poetry Review, Best American Poetry, Chicago Review, Denver Quarterly, Ecotone, Ploughshares,* and elsewhere. She serves as English-language editor of the global poetry initiative *Duniyaadaari,* and with the poet Amy King, edited *Poets for Living Waters,* an international response to the BP oil disaster in the Gulf of Mexico, with continued sites of action; and *Big Energy Poets: When Ecopoetry Thinks Climate Change* (BlazeVOX, 2018). She lives with her partner and daughter in the Appalachian Highlands on Ruffner Mountain, neighbors with the imperiled tricolored bat.

AHSAHTA PRESS

NEW SERIES

AHSAHTA PRESS

SAWTOOTH POETRY PRIZE SERIES

This book is set in Apollo MT type
with DIN Bold titles
by Ahsahta Press at Boise State University.
Cover design by Quemadura.
Book design by Janet Holmes.

AHSAHTA PRESS

2018

JANET HOLMES, DIRECTOR

LINDSEY APPELL

PATRICIA BOWEN, *intern*

MICHAEL GREEN

KATHRYN JENSEN

COLIN JOHNSON

MATT NAPLES